DOING MARRIAGE GOD'S WAY

THE FOUNDATIONS

COUPLE'S DISCUSSION AND ACTIVITY GUIDE

JIMMY EVANS

DOING MARRIAGE GOD'S WAY

THE FOUNDATIONS

COUPLE'S DISCUSSION AND ACTIVITY GUIDE

JIMMY EVANS

XO
PUBLISHING

XO
PUBLISHING

ISBN: 978-1-960870-61-2 eBook
ISBN: 978-1-960870-62-9 Paperback

XO Publishing is a leading creator of relationship-based resources. We focus primarily on marriage-related content for churches, small group curriculum, and people looking for timeless truths about relationships and overall marital health. For more information on other resources from XO Publishing, visit XOPublishing.com.

XO Publishing
1021 Grace Lane
Southlake, TX 76092

While the authors make every effort to provide accurate URLs at the time of printing for external or third-party internet websites, neither they nor the publisher assume any responsibility for changes or errors made after publication.

Printed in the United States of America

25 26 27 28—5 4 3 2 1

Table of Contents

Introduction

Welcome to Your Marriage Journey!

This is *your* book—one copy for the two of you to share. Over the next six sessions, you'll watch video teachings together, have guided conversations, complete activities as a couple, and build your marriage on God's foundations.

WHAT YOU'LL NEED:

- ✓ This guide (just one copy!)
- ✓ Video access
- ✓ 6 sessions, which are usually one week apart, with one dedicated evening for each session (90 minutes)
- ✓ A comfortable, private space for just the two of you
- ✓ Honesty and commitment
- ✓ Optional: A separate notebook for each of you for additional notes

HOW THIS WORKS:

Each week follows this flow:

1. **Prepare**—Set the scene for quality time (5 min)
2. **Watch**—Video teaching together (12-15 min)
3. **Discuss**—Guided conversation (30-40 min)
4. **Apply**—Create your action plan (15-20 min)
5. **Commit**—Agree on weekly practices (5 min)
6. **Pray**—Close in prayer together (5 min)

GROUND RULES:

- Phones off, TV off, distractions eliminated.
- Speak *for* yourself, not *about* your spouse.
- Listen to understand, not to fix or defend.
- Both of you get equal airtime.
- Extend grace—you're both learning.
- Remember: *you're on the same team.*

BEFORE YOU BEGIN:

Sit together right now and answer out loud:

Why are we doing this?

Take turns sharing. Each person gets 2 minutes.

What do we hope will be different after six weeks?

Discuss together for 5 minutes.

Your Weekly Time:

Day: _____Time: _____ Location: _____

OPENING PRAYER TOGETHER:

One of you read this aloud, then pray in your own words:

"God, we invite You into this journey. We want to build our marriage Your way. Give us open hearts, honest conversations, and courage to change. Help us become the couple You created us to be. In Jesus' name. Amen."

SESSION 1

The Most Important Decision in Marriage

PREPARE (5 MINUTES)

Environment:

- Choose your spot (couch, porch, dining table).
- Eliminate distractions (phones put away).
- Get comfortable.
- Light a candle if you'd like.

Connection Moment:

Before you start, share one thing you appreciate about your spouse from this past week.

WATCH TOGETHER (15 MINUTES)

As you watch, one person can jot notes here or you can just listen together.

Key Concepts to Listen For:

- The four deepest human needs
- The principle of transference
- The woman at the well
- Where we should take our needs first

DISCUSS (35 MINUTES)

Round 1: The Four Needs (10 minutes)

Jimmy Evans mentioned the four deepest needs: **Acceptance, Identity, Security, Purpose.**

Take turns answering (3 minutes each, then discuss together):

- Which of these four needs do you most often try to get from me?
- Can you think of a recent time when you expected me to meet one of these needs?

Round 2: The Transference Trap (10 minutes)

Jimmy Evans talked about transferring expectations to our spouse that only God can meet.

Discuss together:

- When have we fought because one of us expected the other to "be Jesus"?
- What does that fight usually sound like? (*Be specific.*)
- How would our marriage change if we both took these needs to Jesus first?

Round 3: Personal Relationship with Jesus (15 minutes)

Each person answer (be honest):

- On a scale of 1–10, how strong is your personal relationship with Jesus right now?
- Do you have a daily time with God? If not, what gets in the way?
- Are you willing to commit to daily time with Jesus for the next six weeks?

Activity: The Need Checker

Together, verbally go through each need and identify where you currently look to get it met:

Identity (Who am I?):

- ☐ Spouse's opinion
- ☐ Job performance
- ☐ Children
- ☐ God's truth

Where do you look most? Discuss.

Acceptance (Am I loved?):

- ☐ Spouse's affection
- ☐ Friends
- ☐ Social media
- ☐ God's love

Where do you look most? Discuss.

Security (Am I safe?):

- ☐ Financial status
- ☐ Spouse's mood
- ☐ Circumstances
- ☐ God's faithfulness

Where do you look most? Discuss.

Purpose (Do I matter?):

- ☐ Career success
- ☐ Spouse's appreciation
- ☐ Achievements
- ☐ God's calling

Where do you look most? Discuss.

APPLY (15 MINUTES)

Your Morning Routine:

Discuss and agree: What time will each of you spend personal time with Jesus?

Husband's time: _____ Wife's time: _____

Where? What will you do? (Read Bible, pray, journal, etc.)

This Week's Commitments:

Read these aloud together and both say "I commit":

- ☐ We will each spend 15 minutes with Jesus every morning before our day starts.
- ☐ We will pray specifically for our four deepest needs to be met by God.
- ☐ We will check in mid-week: "How's your Jesus time? What's changing?"
- ☐ We will share one thing on Sunday: "How did Jesus meet a need this week?"

Accountability:

How will you encourage each other? Text mid-morning? Ask at dinner?

Plan: _____

PRAY TOGETHER (5 MINUTES)

Prayer Framework:

Husband prays:

- • Thank God for your wife.
- • Confess where you've expected her to be Jesus.
- • Ask God to meet your four deepest needs.

Wife prays:

- Thank God for your husband.
- Confess where you've expected him to be Jesus.
- Ask God to meet your four deepest needs.

Together:

Hold hands, look into each other's eyes, say "I love you," and then pray the following:

- **Pray for your marriage:** "God, help us build our marriage on You as the foundation. Help us love each other without expecting each other to be our savior."
- **Pray for your morning times:** "Give us discipline and hunger for You. Meet us in our quiet times and fill us with Your presence."
- **Pray for transformation:** "Change our hearts so we turn to You first for our deepest needs. Help us encourage each other's relationship with You."
- **Pray for the coming week:** "Guide us as we practice this new way of living. Help us remember that You are our source."
- **Close with commitment:** Each person says, "I choose to seek Jesus first." Say "Amen" together.

THIS WEEK'S DATE NIGHT

- **Date Idea:** Go for a walk or get coffee. Talk about your spiritual journeys. When did you first meet Jesus? What's your story?
- **Date Night Question:** "What would our marriage look like if we both woke up with our needs already met by Jesus?"

NOTES

_____

_____

_____

_____

_____

_____

_____

_____

_____

_____

_____

_____

_____

_____

_____

_____

_____

_____

SESSION 2

The Law of Priority

Leaving and Cleaving

PREPARE (5 MINUTES)

Before you start, go on a 5-minute walk together or sit outside. Share: "What did you notice this week as you spent time with Jesus?"

WATCH TOGETHER (15 MINUTES)

Key Concepts to Listen For:

- The four laws and where they come from
- What "leave" really means
- Pastor Jimmy's golfing story
- Legitimate jealousy
- Children and priorities

DISCUSS (35 MINUTES)

Round 1: The Time Truth (15 minutes)

Get out your phones and look at your screen time from this past week. Compare numbers. Then discuss:

Together, estimate weekly hours for:

- Focused time with each other: _____ hours
- Work: _____ hours
- Children: _____ hours
- TV/streaming: _____ hours
- Phone/social media: _____ hours
- Hobbies: _____ hours

Now discuss:

- What gets more focused attention than our marriage?
- What story do these numbers tell?
- Are we okay with this story?

Round 2: The Golfing Conversation (10 minutes)

Jimmy hung up his golf clubs to prioritize Karen.

Take turns sharing:

- What might I need to "hang up" to put you first?
- What competes with you for my time, energy, and attention?
- What makes you feel like you're *not* first?

Listen without defending. Just listen and learn.

Round 3: Children Discussion (10 minutes—if applicable)

If you have children, discuss:

- Have our kids taken priority over our marriage? *Be honest.*
- What would our kids say about our marriage? Would they say mom and dad are solid?
- What needs to change?

If you don't have kids yet but plan to, discuss:

- What will we commit to *now* to keep our marriage first when kids come?
- What boundaries will we set?

APPLY (15 MINUTES)

Activity: The Hangup

Husband says:

"To put you first, I will give up or reorganize: _____ ."

Wife says:

"To put you first, I will give up or reorganize: _____ ."

Our Daily Hour:

When and where will you have one hour together daily with no distractions?

Time: _____ Place: _____

Phones will be: _____

If you have kids, they'll be: _____

Our Weekly Date Night:

Commit to a recurring date night right now.

Day: _____ Time: _____

Who plans this week? _____

Will this be recurring, or set week by week? _____

Phone Boundaries:

Agree together:

- During meals: _____
- After _____ PM: _____
- During conversations: _____
- In bed: _____

This Week's Commitments

Read aloud together and both say "I commit":

- ☐ We will protect one hour daily for each other—no phones, no distractions.
- ☐ We will complete our "hangup"—what we said we'd give up or reorganize.
- ☐ We will have our first weekly date night this week.
- ☐ We will honor our phone boundaries.
- ☐ We will have a mid-week check: "Am I feeling like I come first? What can I do better?"

PRAY TOGETHER (5 MINUTES)

Prayer Framework:

- Thank God for bringing you together.
- Confess what you've put before your marriage.
- Ask for discipline to protect your marriage time.
- Commit your priorities to Him.

THIS WEEK'S DATE NIGHT

Date Idea: Go somewhere you went when you were dating. Remember when you naturally prioritized each other.

Date Questions:

- "What did we do when we were dating that we've stopped doing?"
- "What made you feel pursued and prioritized back then?"
- "How can we get that back?"

NOTES

SESSION 3

The Law of Pursuit

Working at Love

PREPARE (5 MINUTES)

Before watching, each person share one way your spouse made you feel prioritized this past week. Be specific.

WATCH TOGETHER (15 MINUTES)

Key Concepts to Listen For:

- What "cleave" means
- Why we fall out of love
- The "Are you okay?" question
- Feelings vs. actions
- Marriage only works when you work at it

DISCUSS (35 MINUTES)

Round 1: The Honesty Hour (10 minutes)

On a scale of 1–10, how would you rate:

- Pursuit in our marriage right now: _____
- My personal effort at pursuing you: _____
- How pursued I feel by you: _____

Share your numbers. Discuss: What do these numbers reveal?

Round 2: The "Are You Okay?" Conversation (15 minutes)

This is the most important conversation of the week. Set a timer for 15 minutes.

Take turns (7 minutes each):

Person 1 asks: "Are you okay? Is there anything I'm not doing? Any need I'm not meeting that you wish I would?"

Person 2 answers honestly while Person 1 just listens—no defending, no explaining.

Then switch roles.

Write down what you heard:

What my spouse said they need: _____ .

Round 3: Dating vs. Now (10 minutes)

Discuss together:

- What did I do to pursue you when we were dating?
- What have I stopped doing?
- What do you miss most from our dating days?
- If I pursued you the way I did back then, what would that look like now?

APPLY (15 MINUTES)

Activity: The Pursuit Plan

This week, I will pursue you by:

Husband commits to:

1. _____

2. _____

3. _____

Wife commits to:

1. _____
2. _____
3. _____

Our Daily "Are You Okay?" Time:

When will you ask each other this question daily?
Time: _____ Place: _____

Feelings vs. Actions Agreement:

Read this aloud together:

> *"We agree that actions come before feelings. We will not wait to 'feel like it' before pursuing each other. We will do the right thing, and the feelings will follow."*

Both say: "I agree."

THIS WEEK'S COMMITMENTS

Read aloud together and both say "I commit":

- ☐ We will each do all three things on our pursuit plan.
- ☐ We will ask "Are you okay?" every single day and really listen.
- ☐ We will protect our daily hour together.
- ☐ We will plan a date that shows pursuit (dress up, effort, thoughtfulness).
- ☐ Mid-week: Check progress and adjust if needed.

PRAY TOGETHER (5 MINUTES)

Prayer Framework:

- Ask God for energy and creativity to pursue each other.
- Confess where you've been lazy.
- Thank your spouse for specific ways they pursue you.
- Ask God to help you serve each other well.

THIS WEEK'S DATE NIGHT

Date Idea: Recreate one of your early dates. Do what you did back then. Dress up. Be intentional. Pursue each other like you did in the beginning.

Date Activity: Share memories from your dating season. Laugh together. Remember the pursuit.

NOTES

_____

_____

_____

_____

_____

_____

_____

_____

_____

_____

_____

_____

_____

_____

_____

_____

_____

_____

_____

SESSION 4

The Law of Partnership

Becoming One

PREPARE (5 MINUTES)

Important: Sit next to each other tonight, not across from each other. You're on the same team.

Before starting, share: "What's one way you pursued me this week that meant a lot?"

WATCH TOGETHER (15 MINUTES)

Key Concepts to Listen For:

- What "one flesh" means
- The 50/50 partnership
- Dominance is gender neutral
- Three names on everything
- The peace test

DISCUSS (35 MINUTES)

Round 1: The Dominance Check (10 minutes)

Discuss honestly:

- On a scale of 1–10, how controlling or dominant am I? (Self-rate.)
- On a scale of 1–10, how controlling or dominant is my spouse? (Cross-rate.)
- Share your numbers and discuss—no defending.

If one person is clearly more dominant:

- Dominant person: Confess it. "I've been controlling in these areas... I'm sorry."
- Other person: Share how it feels to be controlled or not heard as an equal.

Round 2: Partnership Assessment (15 minutes)

Activity: Check Your Partnership

Go through these areas together. Put a checkmark if you truly function as equal partners:

- ☐ Financial decisions
- ☐ Parenting choices
- ☐ Social calendar
- ☐ Household responsibilities
- ☐ Major purchases
- ☐ Career decisions
- ☐ Extended family
- ☐ Spiritual decisions
- ☐ Vacation planning
- ☐ Home decisions

Count your checkmarks: _____ out of 10

Discuss:

- Where are we doing well?
- Where do we need to improve?
- In the unchecked areas, who tends to dominate? Why?

Round 3: "My" vs. "Our" (10 minutes)

Together, identify what you call "mine" that should be "ours". Circle the check mark if this is language you use, or the X if it isn't.

- Our money (not "my money"): ✓ or X
- Our car(s) (not "my car"): ✓ or X
- Our children (not "my kids"): ✓ or X
- Our families (not "my family"): ✓ or X
- Our home (not "my house"): ✓ or X
- Our decisions (not "my choice"): ✓ or X

Discuss:

Where do we need to change our language and thinking?

APPLY (15 MINUTES)

Activity: The Partnership Agreement

Read this aloud together, filling in the blanks:

"We agree that we are equal 50/50 partners in everything."

Decisions requiring mutual agreement and peace:

- Purchases over $_____
-
-
-

We will pray together about:

- Major financial decisions
-
-

"We commit to the Peace Test: We will never make a major decision unless we *both* have peace from God."

Both sign:

Husband: _____ Date: _____

Wife: _____ Date: _____

The Peace Test Practice:

Is there a decision you need to make right now?

Decision: _____

Do you both have peace about it? Yes _____ No _____ Not sure _____

If no or not sure: Commit to pray about it daily this week and discuss again on Sunday.

THIS WEEK'S COMMITMENTS

Read aloud together and both say "I commit":

- ☐ We will practice saying "our" instead of "my."
- ☐ The more dominant person will consciously defer to the other.
- ☐ We will pray together about one decision we need to make.
- ☐ We will honor our partnership agreement.
- ☐ We will check in mid-week: "Am I honoring our partnership? What can I do better?"

PRAY TOGETHER (5 MINUTES)

Prayer Framework:

- ◆ Confess any dominance or control.
- ◆ Thank God for making you equal partners.
- ◆ Ask for humility and mutual submission.
- ◆ Pray for God's peace to guide your decisions.

THIS WEEK'S DATE NIGHT

Date Idea: Go to a nice restaurant. Bring this book. Practice the Peace Test together by discussing a decision you've been putting off. Don't leave until you both have peace.

Bonus: Try ordering for each other for one meal. Practice partnership even in small things.

NOTES

SESSION 5

The Law of Purity

Creating Safety

PREPARE (5 MINUTES)

Important: Have tissues ready. This session can be emotional. Sit close. Hold hands. Remember you're both on a journey of growth.

Before starting, share: "What did you appreciate about being equal partners this week?"

WATCH TOGETHER (15 MINUTES)

Key Concepts to Listen For:

- Naked and unashamed
- Fig leaves and hiding
- Power of the tongue
- Pastor Jimmy's verbal abuse story
- Taking responsibility
- The wages of sin

DISCUSS (40 MINUTES)

Round 1: The Safety Check (10 minutes)

On a scale of 1–10, discuss together:

- How safe do I feel to share my thoughts honestly with you? ____
- How safe do I feel to be emotionally vulnerable with you? ____
- How safe do I feel to be physically open with you? ____
- Share your numbers. Ask: "What would make you feel safer with me?"

Listen without defending. Just receive.

Round 2: Fig Leaves (15 minutes)

Fig leaves are the ways we hide from each other.

Together, identify your fig leaves:

Do we hide by:

- Avoiding honest conversations? Yes / No
- Keeping emotions to ourselves? Yes / No
- Being physically distant? Yes / No
- Staying busy so we don't have to connect? Yes / No
- Using humor or sarcasm to deflect? Yes / No
- Using kids as buffers? Yes / No
- Keeping secrets (even small ones)? Yes / No

For each "yes," discuss: Why do we hide in this way? What are we protecting?

Round 3: Taking Responsibility (15 minutes)

This is hard but crucial.

Each person takes 7 minutes (set a timer):

Share one specific way you've sinned against your spouse that you haven't fully owned or apologized for.

Use these exact words:

"I'm sorry for _____. I was wrong. Will you forgive me?"

Be specific:

- "I'm sorry for how I spoke to you when..."
- "I'm sorry for shutting down instead of..."
- "I'm sorry for putting _____ before you..."

The listener says:

"I forgive you. Thank you for taking responsibility."

Then switch roles.

APPLY (15 MINUTES)

Activity: Practice the Phrase

Right now, practice saying this three times to each other:

"I'm sorry. I was wrong. Will you forgive me?"

Take turns. Say it for real things (even small). Practice until it feels natural.

Our Purity Commitments:

Read aloud together:

"We commit to creating safety in our marriage by:

- Taking responsibility when we mess up
- Saying 'I'm sorry. I was wrong. Will you forgive me?' immediately
- Guarding our mouths—speaking life, not death
- Being honest even when it's hard
- Removing one fig leaf this week."

The Fig Leaf We'll Remove:

One area where we'll be more vulnerable and open this week:

_____

How we'll support each other:

_____

THIS WEEK'S COMMITMENTS

Read aloud together and both say "I commit":

- ☐ We will say "I'm sorry. I was wrong. Will you forgive me?" every time we mess up.
- ☐ We will remove the fig leaf we identified.
- ☐ We will guard our mouths—no harsh words, criticism, or sarcasm.
- ☐ We will create safety by how we respond when the other is vulnerable.
- ☐ We will ask mid-week: "Do you feel safer with me than last week? What can I do?"

PRAY TOGETHER (10 MINUTES)

Prayer Framework:

This is important. Be vulnerable in prayer.

- Confess out loud specific ways you've sinned against each other.
- Ask God to help you take responsibility.
- Pray for safety to grow in your marriage.
- Thank your spouse for being vulnerable.

THIS WEEK'S DATE NIGHT

Date Idea: Stay home. Light candles. Put on soft music. Have a "naked and unashamed" conversation.

Date Activity: Share something you've never shared before. Be vulnerable. Tell a story from your past, share a fear, reveal something you usually hide. Create safety by listening with love.

NOTES

SESSION 6

God's Blueprint

His Design for Husbands and Wives

PREPARE (5 MINUTES)

Before you begin, share: "What's the most important thing you've learned over the last 5 sessions?"

WATCH TOGETHER (15 MINUTES)

Key Concepts to Listen For:

- Ephesians 5
- Sacrificial servant leader (husband's role)
- Respectful helpmate (wife's role)
- Security and respect
- Sin natures: apathy and independence
- "Would you do that to Jesus?"

READ TOGETHER (5 MINUTES)

Read Ephesians 5:21–33 out loud.

[S]ubmitting to one another in the fear of God.

Wives, submit to your own husbands, as to the Lord. For the husband is head of the wife, as also Christ is head of the church; and He is the Savior of the body. Therefore, just as the church is subject to Christ, so let the wives be to their own husbands in everything.

Husbands, love your wives, just as Christ also loved the church and gave Himself for her, that He might sanctify and cleanse her with the washing of water by the word, that He might present her to Himself a glorious church, not having spot or wrinkle or any such thing, but that she should be holy and without blemish. So husbands ought to love their own wives as their own bodies; he who loves his wife loves himself. For no one ever hated his own flesh, but nourishes and cherishes it, just as the Lord does the church. For we are members of His body, of His flesh and of His bones. "For this reason a man shall leave his father and mother and be joined to his wife, and the two shall become one flesh." This is a great mystery, but I speak concerning Christ and the church. Nevertheless let each one of you in particular so love his own wife as himself, and let the wife see that she respects her husband.

After reading, share: "What stands out? What challenges you?"

DISCUSS (30 MINUTES)

Round 1: Gut Reaction (10 minutes)

Be completely honest:
- What's your initial reaction to biblical roles?
- What excites you? What bothers you?
- What questions do you have?

Discuss openly. It's okay to wrestle with this.

Round 2: Security and Respect (10 minutes)

Wife shares (5 minutes):
- On a scale of 1–10, how secure do I feel in our marriage? _____
- What makes me feel secure?
- What makes me feel insecure?

Husband shares (5 minutes):

- On a scale of 1–10, how respected do I feel? _____
- What makes me feel respected?
- What makes me feel disrespected?

Round 3: Sin Natures (10 minutes)

Discuss together:

For wives: Can you see the sin nature of independence in your marriage?

- Acting without including your husband?
- Making decisions alone?
- Dismissing his input?

For husbands: Can you see the sin nature of apathy in your marriage?

- Being passive?
- Checking out?
- Not fighting for the relationship?

Both: How have our sin natures hurt our marriage?

APPLY (20 MINUTES)

Activity: The Role Commitment

Wife Answers:

- If Jesus were my husband, how would I treat Him differently?

  _____

- One way I'll honor my husband this week:

  _____

- When I'm tempted toward independence, I will:

  _____

Husband Answers:

- If I loved my wife like my own body, what would change?

  _____

- One way I'll sacrificially love my wife this week:

  _____

- When I'm tempted toward apathy, I will:

  _____

Our Role Agreement:

Read aloud together:

"We commit to fulfilling our biblical roles:

Husband commits: To be a sacrificial servant leader who lays down his life for his wife, fights for the marriage, and makes her feel secure.

Wife commits: To be a respectful helpmate who honors her husband, includes him in decisions, and makes him feel respected.

Both commit: To submit to one another out of reverence for Christ."

Sign here:

Husband: _____ Date: _____

Wife: _____ Date: _____

THIS WEEK'S COMMITMENTS

Read aloud together and both say "I commit":

- ☐ **Wife:** I will honor my husband in one specific way daily.
- ☐ **Husband:** I will sacrificially love my wife in one specific way daily.
- ☐ Each evening, we'll ask: "Did you feel honored/secure today?"
- ☐ We will read Ephesians 5:21–33 together again this weekend.
- ☐ Mid-week: Discuss how we're doing with our roles.

PRAY TOGETHER (5 MINUTES)

Prayer Framework:

- Thank God for His design for marriage.
- Ask God to help you fulfill your role.
- Confess where your sin nature has hurt your marriage.
- Commit to crucifying your sin nature and serving each other.

THIS WEEK'S DATE NIGHT

Date Idea: Celebrate! Go somewhere special. Dress up.

Date Questions:

- "How have you seen me grow in the last 6 weeks?"
- "What do you love most about us doing this together?"
- "What's different about us now?"
- "Where do we go from here?"

NOTES

Course Completion

Building Your Future Together

Celebrate!

You did it! You made an intentional investment in your marriage. Well done!

Reflection Questions:

Discuss together:

- What was the hardest session? Why?
- What was the most transformative session? Why?
- What's different about us now compared to before we took this course together?

THE FOUR LAWS REVIEW

Together, rate yourselves on each law (1–10):

1. **Priority**—Marriage comes first (except God)
   Our rating: _____ / 10
   What we're doing well: _____
   What needs work: _____

2. **Pursuit**—Work energetically at the relationship
   Our rating: _____ / 10
   What we're doing well: _____
   What needs work: _____

3. **Partnership**—Equal partners in everything
   Our rating: _____ / 10
   What we're doing well: _____
   What needs work: _____

4. **Purity**—Take responsibility for behavior
   Our rating: _____ / 10
   What we're doing well: _____
   What needs work: _____

YOUR 90-DAY MARRIAGE PLAN

Our Priority Law:

Based on your ratings, which law needs the most attention in the next 90 days?

We choose: _____

Our Specific Action Plan:

Daily, we will:

_____

Weekly, we will:

_____

Monthly, we will:

_____

Our Weekly Marriage Check-In:

Day: _____ Time: _____ Place: _____

What we'll do during this time:

- Review our progress on our priority law.
- Ask "Are you okay?"
- Rate each law (1–10).
- Pray together.
- Adjust as needed.

YOUR MARRIAGE COVENANT

Read this out loud together, then sign below:

"We covenant before God to build our marriage on His foundations.

We will:

- Trust Jesus with our four deepest needs, taking them to Him first.
- Keep our marriage as the top priority after God.
- Pursue each other energetically for the rest of our lives.
- Function as equal partners, making decisions together in God's peace.
- Take responsibility for our behavior and create a safe environment.
- Fulfill our biblical roles with sacrificial love and respectful honor.
- Keep growing, learning, and investing in our marriage.

We recognize that marriage is work, but it's the best work we'll ever do. With God's help, we will build something beautiful together that honors Him and blesses others."

Signed:

Husband: _____ Date: _____

Wife: _____ Date: _____

WHERE DO WE GO FROM HERE?

Immediate Next Steps:

Check what you'll do:

- ☐ Put our weekly check-in on the calendar for the next 3 months.
- ☐ Schedule our next date night.
- ☐ Buy one recommended book to read together.
- ☐ Find another couple to mentor using this course.
- ☐ Sign up for a marriage conference.
- ☐ Continue in marriage coaching/counseling.
- ☐ Start another marriage study.
- ☐ Join a couples small group.

Resources We'll Explore:

Circle one to start with:

- *The Four Laws of Love* by Jimmy Evans

- *Marriage on the Rock* by Jimmy Evans

- Marriage conferences and retreats

NON-NEGOTIABLES

Read these aloud together and commit:

We will maintain these practices:

- **Daily:** Personal time with Jesus (individually)
- **Daily:** "Are you okay?" conversation
- **Daily:** One hour face-to-face with no distractions
- **Weekly:** Date night
- **Weekly:** Marriage check-in using material from this course
- **Monthly:** Review the four laws together
- **Yearly:** Marriage retreat or getaway

A LETTER TO YOUR FUTURE SELVES

Write this together. Open it in one year.

Date: _____

Dear Us in One Year,

Today we finished the "Doing Marriage God's Way" course.

Here's what we learned:

_____

_____

_____

Here's what we're committing to:

_____

_____

_____

Here's what we hope is true a year from now:

_____

_____

_____

We love each other. We're in this together. God is building our house.

Signed, _____ and _____

Seal this letter. Put it somewhere safe. Open it one year from today.

FINAL PRAYER TOGETHER

Hold hands. Look at each other. Pray together:

Husband, pray:

- Thank God for your wife.
- Pray for your marriage.
- Commit to leading with sacrificial love.

Wife, pray:

- Thank God for your husband.
- Pray for your marriage.
- Commit to honoring with respect.

Together, pray:

"God, thank You for these six weeks. Thank You for Your design for marriage. Help us keep growing, keep pursuing, keep prioritizing. Build our house on the Rock. We trust You. In Jesus' name. Amen."

Kiss each other. Celebrate your commitment.

Appendix

Quick Reference

THE FOUR DEEPEST NEEDS

1. **Acceptance**—Am I loved? (Anchor in God)
2. **Identity**—Who am I? (Anchor in God)
3. **Security**—Am I safe? (Anchor in God)
4. **Purpose**—Do I matter? (Anchor in God)

THE FOUR LAWS OF MARRIAGE

1. **Priority**—Marriage comes first (except God)
2. **Pursuit**—Work energetically at the relationship
3. **Partnership**—Equal partners (50/50)
4. **Purity**—Take responsibility for behavior

BIBLICAL ROLES

- **Both:** Submit to one another (Eph 5:21).
- **Wives:** Respect and honor your husband.
- **Husbands:** Love your wife sacrificially.

WEEKLY CHECK-IN QUESTIONS

1. Rate each law 1–10. Where are we strong? Where do we need work?
2. Are you okay? Any unmet needs?
3. Did you feel prioritized this week?
4. Did I pursue you well?
5. Did you feel like an equal partner?
6. Did you feel safe with me?
7. What can I do better this week?

EMERGENCY RESET PHRASES

- "I'm sorry. I was wrong. Will you forgive me?"
- "Help me understand your perspective."
- "Are you okay?"
- "We're on the same team."
- "What's most important to you here?"

Final Word

Marriage is a marathon, not a sprint.

These six sessions are just the beginning. The real work is in the daily discipline of living out what you've learned.

Jimmy and Karen Evans almost divorced at 22. Look at them now at 70+—deeply in love, thriving, helping millions.

That can be you.

Build on these foundations. Stay the course. Keep growing together.

And remember: **"Unless the LORD builds the house, the builders labor in vain."** (Psalm 127:1)

Let God build your house.

Therefore encourage one another and build each other up, just as in fact you are doing.

—1 Thessalonians 5:11

www.ingramcontent.com/pod-product-compliance
Lightning Source LLC
Chambersburg PA
CBHW081644040426
42449CB00015B/3447